DATE DUE

MAY 2 5 2001		
JUN 2 7 2001		
MAY 0 9 2007		
FEB 0 2 2011		
FEB 0 4 2012		

THE MAN WHO MADE PARKS

The Story of Parkbuilder Frederick Law Olmsted

THE MAN WHO MADE PARKS

The Story of Parkbuilder Frederick Law Olmsted

FRIEDA WISHINSKY ⸙ *Illustrated by* **SONG NAN ZHANG**

Tundra Books

For my friends Melanie Colbert and Karen Klockner
F.W.

For the parkbuilders of yesterday, today, and tomorrow
S.N.Z.

Text copyright ©1999 by Frieda Wishinsky
Illustrations copyright ©1999 by Song Nan Zhang

Published in Canada by Tundra Books, *McClelland & Stewart Young Readers*,
481 University Avenue, Toronto, Ontario M5G 2E9

Published in the United States by Tundra Books of Northern New York,
P.O. Box 1030, Plattsburgh, New York 12901

Library of Congress Catalog Number: 98-75029

Canadian Cataloguing in Publication Data

Wishinsky, Frieda
The man who made parks : the story of parkbuilder Frederick Law Olmsted

ISBN 0-88776-435-5

1. Olmsted, Frederick Law, 1822-1903 – Juvenile literature.   2. Central Park (New York, N.Y.) – History – Juvenile literature.   3. Parks – United States – History – Juvenile literature.   4. Parks – Canada – History – Juvenile literature.   5. Landscape architects – United States – Biography – Juvenile literature.   I. Zhang, Song Nan, 1942– .   II. Title.

SB470.O5W57 1999   j712'.092   C98-932430-3

We acknowledge the support of the Canada Council for the Arts and the Ontario Arts Council for our publishing program.

We acknowledge the financial support of the Government of Canada through the Book Publishing Industry Development Program for our publishing activities.

Design by Ingrid Paulson
Printed and bound in Canada

1 2 3 4 5 6   04 03 02 01 00 99

Close your eyes.

Imagine yourself in a city park.

Soft grass carpets your feet.

Wildflowers sway in the breeze.

Towering trees surround you.

Once there were no city parks. Many children grew up surrounded by dust and mud, stone and brick. They lived in small, dark, crowded apartments. They played on dirty, treeless streets, dodging horses and garbage. The air crackled with the clatter of hooves and the shouts of vendors.

There was no place to escape until a man named Frederick Law Olmsted changed cities forever.

Frederick Law Olmsted was born in Hartford, Connecticut in 1822. As a young boy, he loved to wander over the rolling hills and valleys of the beautiful New England countryside. His wandering days ended, however, when he was sent away to boarding school. Frederick hated the overbearing schoolmasters and harsh regime, and longed to go home.

One summer, to his relief, a bad bout of poison sumac prevented him from returning to school. He was free to wander again – meandering down quiet country paths lined with brilliant wildflowers, watching cattle graze in the fields, listening to the rustle of trees and the sweet song of birds.

Although Frederick hadn't liked the confinement of school, he loved to read and learn. He read books in his father's library, especially those about the magnificent parks and gardens in England. Frederick thought they were beautiful. He became so interested in parks, he suggested his father plant more trees on their property to improve the view.

Though he didn't realize it then, Frederick had designed his first park. It would be many years before he did so again.

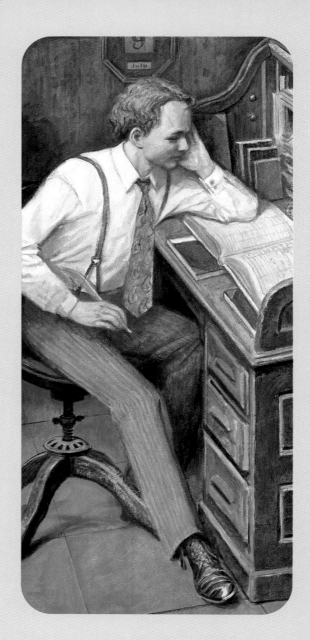

When his formal education ended, Frederick drifted from one career to another. At sixteen he became a surveyor, mapping and measuring land. At eighteen he worked in a New York import business, sitting on a stool for hours, adding long columns of numbers. At twenty he sailed aboard the clipper, the *Ronaldson*, bound for China. At twenty-four he worked as a farmer. But none of those professions suited Frederick, or made him happy.

Then Frederick heard that his adored younger brother, John, planned to embark on a walking tour of England for his health. Frederick begged to join him. Together they roamed the English countryside, reveling in the beauty of the landscape.

Near Liverpool, Frederick viewed his first public park – Birkenhead, the "People's Park." He was enchanted by its winding paths, open fields, lakes, bridges, and summerhouses. Most of all he loved the fact that the park was open to all the residents of the city. He later wrote: "All this magnificent pleasure ground is entirely, unreservedly, and forever, the people's own."

When Frederick returned home, he wrote a book about his trip to England. He enjoyed writing so much, he left farming and became a newspaper reporter for the *New York Daily Times*. As a reporter, Frederick traveled to the southern United States and wrote moving accounts of the terrible conditions arising from slavery. He also wrote articles about the difficulties new immigrants faced in New York City. Not long after, he became a magazine publisher.

When his magazine failed, Frederick was again at a loss. What direction should his life take? For years his family had been understanding about his career changes, but he was now thirty-five. He couldn't keep drifting; he had to find a profession that suited him. The question was, what?

The answer came through a chance conversation.

As Frederick had written in his articles, New York was teeming with immigrants. Many lived in poverty, breathing foul air and living in squalid, crowded, unhealthy tenements. A movement to create a park in the city had begun years before, but had stalled because of arguments about the park's location. Finally, 840 miserable acres in the sparsely populated center of Manhattan were set aside. A few men, including Charles Elliot, were put in charge of organizing the project.

In 1857 Frederick met Charles Elliot, by chance, at an inn in Connecticut, and was immediately caught up with the idea of building a park for New York. Finally New York would have a green space for all its people, rich and poor, young and old, just like beautiful Birkenhead Park in England!

"Why don't you apply for the job of park superintendent?" Charles Elliot suggested to Frederick. Charles went on to explain that the superintendent would be in charge of cleaning up the land where the park would be built. The land was a mess! It was rocky and swampy, with pigsties and slaughterhouses everywhere. It was filthy and smelled disgusting, but none of that bothered Frederick. In his imagination, the park's transformation had already begun.

When Frederick arrived at the park site to meet his new boss and chief engineer, Egbert Viele, he was brimming with enthusiasm and ideas. But Egbert shared neither. He thought Frederick was an impractical dreamer who would be useless doing real work on real land. To prove his point, he sent Frederick out with a snarly workman named Mr. Hawkins.

Mr. Hawkins took Frederick on a hike through the muckiest, muddiest sections of the park site. Frederick hadn't expected a hike and wasn't dressed for one. His clean pants sank deep into the dirt and slime. Mr. Hawkins and the workmen could barely stop themselves from laughing. All Frederick could do was grit his teeth and keep walking.

Despite Egbert's attitude, Frederick was determined to succeed at his new position. The next time he visited the site, he wore rough workman's clothes and heavy boots. He organized the men into teams and told them he expected them to work hard. He insisted on hiring more workers, and even waded right into the muck and mud to ensure the work was done properly.

Soon the swamps on the park site were drained. The pigsties and slaughterhouses were leveled. The land was cleared. No one laughed at Frederick anymore. The workmen respected and admired his good sense and hard work.

Now that the site had been cleared, it was time to design the park. The park commissioners wanted something imaginative. Original. Charming. Where would the design come from?

They'd hold a competition! The winner would receive two thousand dollars and the opportunity to design Central Park.

One of the people interested in entering the competition was gifted architect Calvert Vaux. Calvert, an expert on designing buildings, invited Frederick, who knew every inch of the park site, to collaborate with him. Calvert was convinced that together they could design something unique and wonderful.

At first Frederick hesitated. His full-time job as park superintendent was tiring and consuming. He was also concerned that, should he collaborate with Calvert, he'd be competing against his boss, Egbert Viele. Egbert told Frederick coldly that it didn't matter one bit to him if Frederick entered the competition. Egbert was confident that Frederick had no hope of winning. As soon as he heard Egbert's harsh words, Frederick knew what he wanted to do: he would design Central Park with Calvert!

The two men worked night after night, drawing on great sheets of paper that covered their table and cascaded to the floor. Sometimes they rode into the park and worked by moonlight, analyzing and measuring the land.

Hour after exhausting hour, they worked. Sometimes they argued. Frederick envisioned the park as a tranquil place for people to escape the bustle and noise of the city. Calvert saw it as a work of art. Despite their differences, they developed a plan that would bring the serenity and beauty of the countryside to the city.

They finished a day before the deadline. All that remained was the decision on the winning design.

On April 28, 1858, by a vote of seven to four, Frederick Law Olmsted and Calvert Vaux were named the official designers of Central Park.

Soon the park began buzzing with workmen. Bricks, gravel, grass, soil, and even dynamite were hauled in. Roadbuilders constructed walkways for people, paths for horses and riders, and lanes for carriages. Bridges were built allowing traffic to flow both over and under. Roads were curved, making the narrow land appear wider. The south section of the park was shaped into rolling pastures, like an English countryside, while the north end's wilder, more rugged landscape was accented and preserved.

And when winter arrived and the lake in the park froze, skaters came to glide and dance on the ice.

§ § §

Soon people everywhere were drawn to the beauty of Central Park. Its fame spread throughout North America, and people clamored for Fred and Calvert to build parks in their cities too.

Frederick Law Olmsted had finally found his career. He was a "landscape architect," a term he and Calvert invented to describe their work.

Over the years, they designed many parks, including Prospect Park in Brooklyn – a place of stately trees and rolling open fields. After their partnership ended, Frederick continued to design parks alone. One of his boldest designs was the Emerald Necklace in Boston – a whole park system circling the shoreline in a ribbon of green.

For over one hundred years, people's lives have been enriched by Frederick's dreams.
Frederick Law Olmsted designed many magnificent public spaces all over North America.

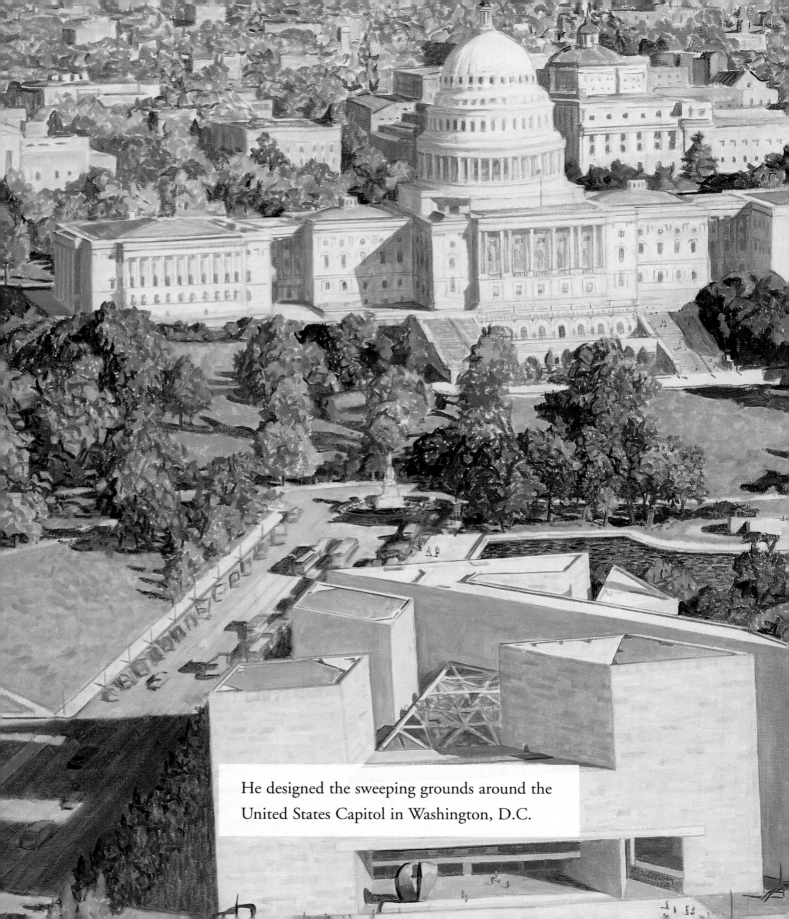

He designed the sweeping grounds around the
United States Capitol in Washington, D.C.

He provided plans for majestic Mount Royal in Montreal, Quebec.

He cleaned up the run-down area around Niagara Falls
and designed a park around its rim.

He proposed that the beautiful Yosemite Valley in California be preserved forever as a national park.

When Frederick Law Olmsted died in 1903, he left magnificent parks all over North America. His glorious idea that every city needs a beating green heart, a place of rest and tranquillity, lives on.